FUNNY JOKES

For 15 YEAR OLD TEENS

COOPER THE POOPER

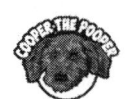

Copyright 2023 © Cooper the Pooper. All rights reserved.

The content contained within this book may not be reproduced, duplicated or transmitted without direct written permission from the author or the publisher.

Under no circumstances will any blame or legal responsibility be held against the publisher, or author, for any damages, reparation, or monetary loss due to the information contained within this book, either directly or indirectly.

Legal Notice:

This book is copyright protected. It is only for personal use. You cannot amend, distribute, sell, use, quote or paraphrase any part, or the content within this book, without the consent of the author or publisher.

Disclaimer Notice:

Please note the information contained within this document is for educational and entertainment purposes only. All effort has been executed to present accurate, up to date, reliable, complete information. No warranties of any kind are declared or implied. Readers acknowledge that the author is not engaged in the rendering of legal, financial, medical or professional advice. The content within this book has been derived from various sources. Please consult a licensed professional before attempting any techniques outlined in this book.

By reading this document, the reader agrees that under no circumstances is the author responsible for any losses, direct or indirect, that are incurred as a result of the use of the information contained within this document, including, but not limited to, errors, omissions, or inaccuracies.

A Message from the Publisher

Hello! My name is Cooper, my Owner and I would like to thank you for buying our book. We have poured our hearts into making books that will inspire young minds and bring smiles to their faces.

It is our sincere hope that you and your aspiring comedian enjoyed this book. If it brought you a bit of laughter or some smiles, **we would be extremely grateful if you could take a moment to share your honest thoughts through an Amazon review**. Your feedback means the world to us, especially as a small business striving to make an impact.

If this book didn't quite hit the mark for you, please don't hesitate to let us know the reasons in your review. We value your insight as it will help us improve and serve you better in the future.

Our mission at Books by Cooper is to create top-notch content that fuels imagination and laughter. But our mission wouldn't be possible without amazing readers (like you) who support us every step of the way.

From the bottom of our hearts, thank you for your purchase. We couldn't do it without you.

With warm regards,
Cooper (and his Owner)

TABLE OF CONTENTS

Introduction vii

    Q & A Jokes 1

    One-Liners 19

    Dad Jokes 27

    Knock-Knock Jokes 39

    Classical Music Jokes 49

    Riddles 55

    Dark Humor 63

Conclusion 89

INTRODUCTION

Get ready for a journey filled with laughs!

Laughter is a magical thing, isn't it? Jokes have the power of bringing people together, laughing is one of life's greatest joys.

What do you call a potato wearing glasses?

Which rapper takes the most naps?

My friend told a knock-knock joke about dishes that made me laugh so hard I couldn't breathe (It's in here, can you find it?)

In this book, you'll discover a treasure trove of the funniest jokes we know – the kind that will make anyone crack a smile. Perfect for making your friends giggle and maybe even some grown-ups (the fun ones).

PS. If you have jokes that are even better – the kind that have you laughing so hard you can't catch your breath – leave it in your review. We'd love to hear your joke.

Q & A JOKES

What do you call security guards who work outside Samsung shops?

Guardians of the Galaxy.

What happened when the world's tongue-twister champion got arrested?

They gave him a tough sentence.

Why do rappers need umbrellas?

Fo'drizzle.

Why are peppers the best at archery?

Because they habanero.

Why did the hipster burn his mouth?

He drank coffee before it was cool.

What state is known for its tiny beverages?

Minnesota.

MINNESOTA

2 | FUNNY JOKES FOR 15 YEAR OLD TEENS

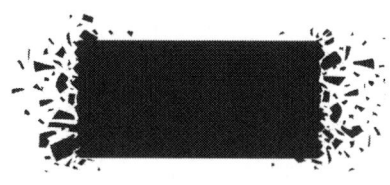

Did you hear about the square that got into a car accident?

Yeah, now he's a rect-angle.

Why did the fart miss graduation?

It got expelled.

Why did the baker have smelly hands?

Because he kneaded a poo!

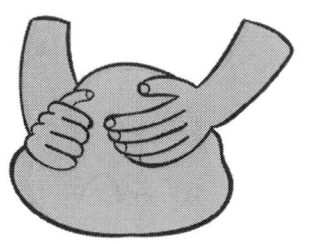

Why did the broom decide to go to bed?

It was very sweepy.

What did the three-legged dog say when he walked into the saloon?

"I'm lookin' for the man who shot my paw."

Why did the computer get mad at the printer?

Because it just didn't like its toner voice.

Do you know where the word "studying" comes from?

Students—dying.

What do you call a 60-year-old who hasn't reached puberty?

A late boomer.

Why were they called the Dark Ages?

Because there were a lot of Knights.

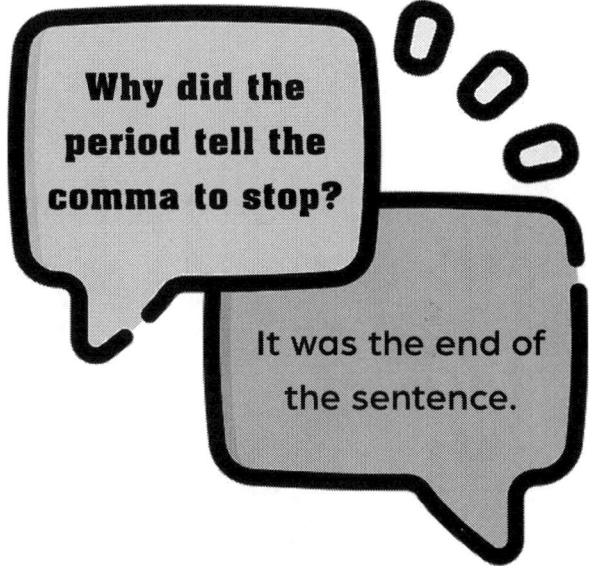

Why did the period tell the comma to stop?

It was the end of the sentence.

What do you call someone who refuses to fart in public?

A private tutor.

Why did the taxi driver get fired?

Passengers didn't like it when she went the extra mile.

How do you tell the difference between a bull and a cow?

It's either one or the udder.

Did you get a hair cut?

No, I got them all cut.

What did one butt cheek say to the other?

"Together, we can stop this crap."

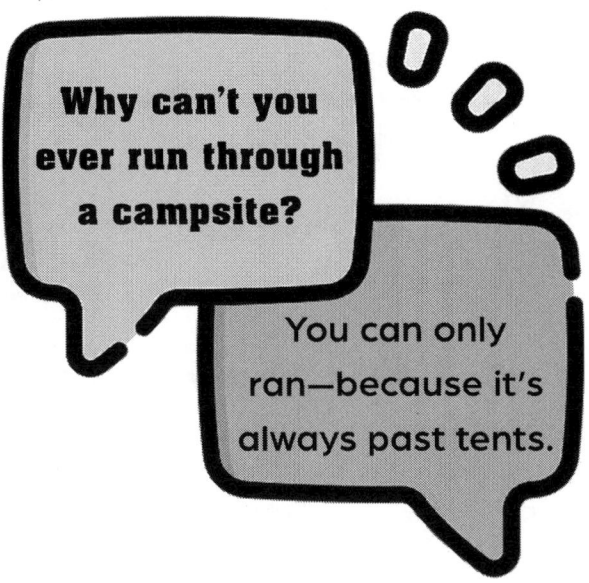

Why can't you ever run through a campsite?

You can only ran—because it's always past tents.

Why did the teacher put on sunglasses?

Because her students were so bright.

Why did the toilet paper roll down the hill?

To get to the bottom.

What do hamburgers call their prom?

The Meat Ball.

Why is it hard to understand volunteers?

Because they make no cents.

Why does Peter Pan always fly?

Because he never lands.

What did the punching bag say to the boxer?

Hit me baby one more time.

What is the easiest way to burn 1,000 calories?

Leave the pizza in the oven.

Why are people always tired in April?

Because they just finished a March!

What do you call a hippie's wife?

Missus-Sippi.

What is the longest word in English?

"Smiles," because there is a whole mile between each "s".

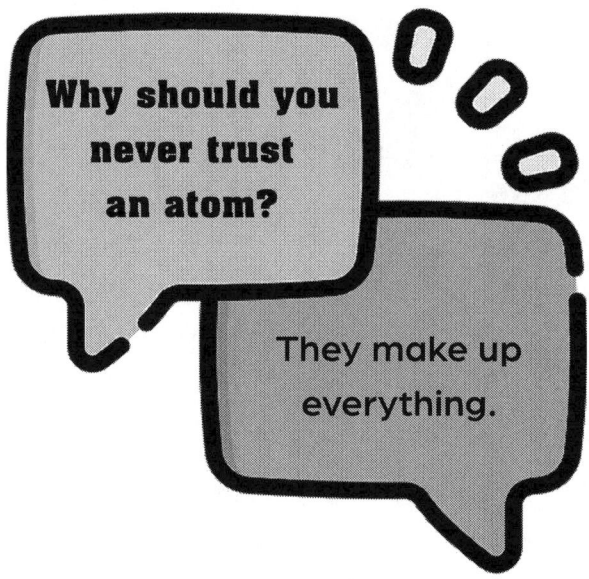

Why should you never trust an atom?

They make up everything.

How can you make a tissue dance?

You just drop a little boogie on it.

What did the drummer call his twin daughters?

Anna one, Anna two.

What do you call a belt with a watch on it?

It is just a waist of time.

What sits in a corner but travels around the world?

A stamp.

Did you hear the joke about the roof?

Never mind, it is over your head.

What is the difference between a badly dressed kid on a bicycle and a well-dressed kid on a tricycle?

Attire.

Where do fruits go on vacation?

Pearis.

What's the difference between a dad joke and a bad joke?

The direction of the first letter.

Why did Adele cross the road?

To sing, "Hello from the other side!"

What did the grape say when it was pinched by the bully?

Nothing. It just gave a little wine.

What's the difference between a hippo and a zippo?

One is very heavy, the other is a little lighter.

What did the Buddhist say to the hot dog vendor?

Make me one with everything.

Which part of the eye is responsible for learning?

The pupil.

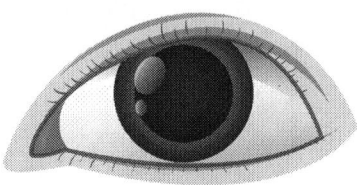

What does a booger tell its true love?

I'm stuck on you.

What did the envelope say to the stamp?

Just stick with me and we will go places.

What is the difference between boogers and broccoli?

Kids don't eat broccoli.

What do you call a sleeping Easter egg?

Egg-zosted.

What day does an Easter egg hate the most?

Fry-day!

Why did the teen run around his bed?

He was trying to catch up on sleep.

What do you find inside a clean nose?

 Fingerprints.

How do you find Will Smith in the snow?

Look for the fresh prints.

 **How can you make the Easter preparations go faster?**

Just use the eggs-press-lane.

Are you free tomorrow?

No, I am expensive.

What do you call a *Star Wars* droid that takes the long way around?

R2-Detour.

What's the difference between roast beef and pea soup?

Anyone can roast beef, but no one can pee soup.

What do you call an egg from outer space?

An egg-stra-terrestrial.

What do you call an old snowman?

A creek.

What do you call a naughty Easter egg?

A practical yolker.

Did you hear about the man who invented the knock, knock joke?

He won the No-bell prize.

ONE-LINERS

Me: I cleaned all the dishes.

Mom: Aren't you gonna put them away too?

Me: You have to upgrade from the trial version to the paid version for that.

I have a joke about chemistry, but I don't think I will get a reaction.

My printer's name is Bob Marley. Because it's always jammin'.

I had a joke about banking, but I lost interest.

When my name is in a math problem and the whole class stares:

Me: That's right b*tches, I bought 60 watermelons.

I have a joke about cows, but I don't want to milk it.

I'm a photographer of myself. You could say, I'm selfie-employed.

Stop looking for that perfect match— use a lighter.

I can kayak. Canoe?

A science teacher tells his class, "Oxygen is vital for breathing and life. It was discovered in 1773."

Timmy responds, "Thank God I was born after 1773! Otherwise, I would have died without it!"

Some kids told me they'd give me $20 to hang out with them. Turns out it was just clique bait.

Finally, my winter fat is gone and I now have spring rolls.

Two artists had an art contest. It ended in a draw.

"Just say no to drugs!"

"Well, if I am talking to my drugs, I probably already said 'yes'".

Imagine if you walked into a bar and there was a long line of people waiting to take a swing at you. That's the punch line.

My wife and I were out to dinner and the waitress started flirting with me.

"She obviously has COVID," observed my wife.

"Why do you say that?" I asked alarmedly.

My wife dryly replied, "Because she has no taste."

I heard Sony's coming out with a new console during the pandemic. It's called the Plaguestation 5.

Give a man a plane ticket and he flies for the day. Push him out of the plane at 3,000 feet and he'll fly for the rest of his life.

I was in Russia listening to a stand-up comedian making jokes about Putin. The jokes weren't that funny, but I liked the execution.

Never criticize someone until you've walked a mile in their shoes. That way, when you criticize them, you'll be a mile away, and you'll have their shoes.

You don't need a parachute to go skydiving. You need a parachute to go skydiving twice.

A hamburger walks into a bar and orders a beer. The bartender says, "Sorry, we don't serve food here."

DAD JOKES

I love dad jokes, but I don't have kids, which makes me a faux pa.

I only know 25 letters of the alphabet—I just don't know y.

My dream job is to clean mirrors. I can see myself doing that my whole life.

I lost 25% of my roof last night... oof.

I don't trust stairs. They're always up to something.

Two peanuts went walking down the street. One was as-salt-ed.

Last night I dreamt that I weighed less than a thousandth of a gram. I was like, 0mg!

6:30 is my favorite time of the day, hands down.

I used to run a dating service for chickens, but I struggled to make hens meet.

My toddler is refusing to nap. He's guilty of resisting a rest.

I'm reading an anti-gravity book and I just can't put it down.

Most people can't tell the difference between entomology and etymology. I can't find the words for how much this bugs me.

I failed my calculus exam because I was sitting in the middle of identical twins—I couldn't differentiate between them.

A magician was walking down the street and he turned into a store.

I can tolerate algebra, maybe even a little calculus, but geometry is where I draw the line!

We're renovating the house, and the first floor is going great, but the second floor is another story.

We're renovating the house, and the first floor is going great, but the second floor is another story.

At first, I thought my chiropractor wasn't any good, but now I stand corrected.

My therapist told me I have problems expressing my emotions. Can't say I'm surprised.

I used to be able to play piano by ear, but now I have to use my hands.

Every night I have a hard time remembering something, but then it eventually dawns on me.

My boss asked me why I only get sick on work days. I said it must be my weekend immune system.

I was once a personal trainer until I gave a too-weak notice.

I love telling Dad jokes. Sometimes, he even laughs.

Have you heard about the new corduroy pillows? They're making headlines!

I just paid $100 for a belt that doesn't fit—what a huge waist!

I finally watched that documentary on clocks. It was about time.

KNOCK-KNOCK JOKES

Knock knock.
Who's there?
Beets.
Beets who?
Beets me!

Knock knock.
Who's there?
I eat mop.
I eat mop who?
You eat your poo? Gross!

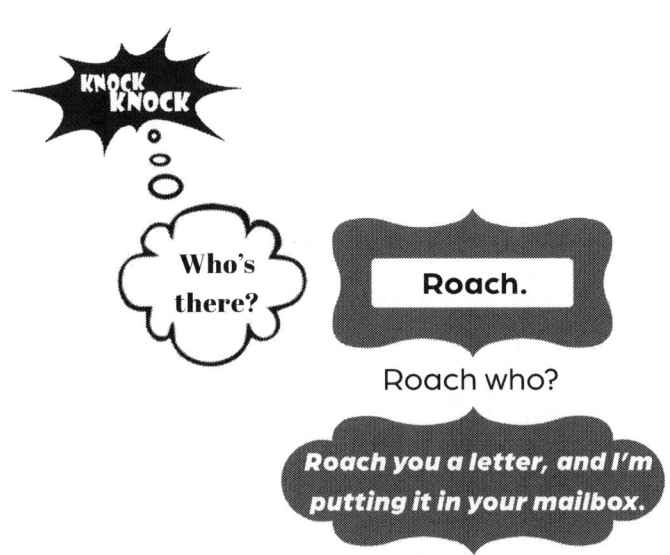

CLASSICAL MUSIC JOKES

My friend spends 75% of his time playing American Football and the other 25% playing Baroque music. I guess you could say he's a quarter Bach!

I went to buy some classical music today... But I forgot my Chopin Liszt.

Do you know that Mozart was a child prodigy? He was A sharp minor.

Want to hear the joke about the staccato in Mozart? Never mind, it's too short.

They say classical music was written to speak through the ages. I guess you could say it is Bach to the future.

Why did the pirate buy a Pavarotti album? Because he loved the high Cs.

Middle C, E flat and G walk into a bar. "Sorry," says the barman. "We don't serve Minors."

How do you fix a broken brass instrument? With a tuba glue.

How can you tell if a singer is at your door? They can't find the key and don't know when to come in.

Classical music should get Bach to basics, because if it isn't Baroque, don't fix it.

My dog loves classical music. Whenever she hears it, she's always Wagner tail.

Earlier today, I heard classical music coming from my wallet. I opened it and found three tenors inside.

I don't think wind turbines even like classical music; I hear they are big metal fans, though.

Killer whales love classical music so much, they form Orcastras.

Why should you never borrow money from a classical pianist? Because they are always Baroque.

If an orchestra plays in a thunderstorm, who is the most likely to get struck by lightning? The conductor, of course!

RIDDLES

What goes up and down, but never moves?

A flight of stairs.

A man builds a house with all four walls facing south. A bear walks past the house. What color is the bear?

White. It is a polar bear.

Two mothers and two daughters go out to eat. Everyone eats a burger, yet, at the end of the evening, only three burgers were eaten in all. How is this possible?

The party consisted of a grandmother, mother, and daughter.

You can find it in a minute or an hour, but never in a day or a month. What is it?

The letter "U".

I am an odd number. Take away one letter and I become even. What number am I?

Seven (take away the "s" and it becomes "even").

You're home alone and fast asleep when your friends come over for breakfast. You have cornflakes, jam, cookies, a carton of milk, and a bottle of juice. What will you open first?

Your eyes.

I wear a crown like a king but my call is disappointing and I have fewer eyes on my face than on my tail. Who am I?

A peacock.

Which English word has three consecutive double letters?

Bookkeeper.

If two's company and three's a crowd, what are five and six?

Eleven.

People walk in and out of me. They push and I follow. When they walk out on me, I clam up. I wait for the next person to walk into my life and then, I open up again. What am I?

An elevator.

What does the letter "T" and an island have in common?

They can both be found in the middle of water.

What word begins and ends with "E" but only has one letter?

Envelope.

What five-letter word becomes shorter when you add two letters to it?

Short.

A man was taking a walk outside when it started to rain. He didn't have an umbrella, and was not wearing a hat so his clothes got soaked. Strangely enough, though, not a single hair on his head got wet. How is this possible?

The man was bald.

A boy was rushed to the ER of the hospital but the attending physician said, "I cannot operate on this boy. He is my son!" But the doctor was not the boy's father. How can this be?

The doctor was the boy's mom.

A boy fell off a 20-foot ladder but did not get hurt. Why not?

He fell from the bottom rung, not the top one.

DARK HUMOR

If someone burns to death, do they get a discount at the crematorium?

A man walks into a library and asks for books about paranoia. The librarian whispers, "They're right behind you!"

I bought my blind friend a cheese grater for his birthday. He later told me it was the most violent book he'd ever read.

Man: How do you prepare your chicken?
Waiter: Nothing special, we just tell them they're gonna die.

My wife left a note on the fridge. "This is not working," but the fridge is working just fine.

Wife: I'm pregnant.
Husband: Hi, pregnant, I'm Dad.
Wife: No, you're not.

Why does Humpty Dumpty love autumn? Because he always has a great fall.

I tried to warn my son about playing Russian Roulette. It went in one ear and out the other.

> Stop elephant poaching. Everyone knows the best way to eat an elephant is grilled.

> Welcome to plastic surgery. It's nice to see so many new faces.

I'm so excited about my new amateur autopsy club. Tuesday is open Mike night!

I'll never forget my dad's last words. "Erase my search history, son."

Why did the man miss the funeral? He wasn't a mourning person.

Doctor: You'll be at peace soon.
Man: Am I dying?
Doctor: No, but your wife is.

When two vegan parents get into an argument, is it still called beef?

Do you know why I hate *The Lion King* song, "I just can't wait to be king"? If you think about it, the song might as well be called, "I just can't wait for my dad to be killed in a stampede."

I asked my girlfriend if I was the only one she'd dated. She said, yes—all the others had been 9s and 10s.

My dad died when we couldn't remember his blood type. As he died, he kept insisting for us to "be positive," but it's hard without him.

What do you call a disease with many followers? Influenza.

Patient: Oh, doctor, I'm just so nervous. This is my first operation.
Doctor: Don't worry, mine too.

If you think I would joke about Alzheimer's, forget it.

A teacher asked students to use "beans" in a sentence. A girl said, "My father grows beans." A boy said, "My mother cooked beans." The student at the back of the class said, "We are all human beans."

I cannot believe there's still no cure for obesity. I thought it would be a walk in the park.

Driver: Sorry, what's the quickest way to get to the hospital?
Pedestrian: Just stand in the middle of a busy road.

What's the special in a restaurant for cannibals? Heads, shoulders, knees, and toes.

After years of drinking, I admit alcohol cures obesity and bad looks. Not in me, in everyone else.

For Sale: Parachute. Used once, never opened, small stain.

What do you call a bacterial disease caused by two grizzlies? Twobearculosis.

A blind woman tells her boyfriend she is seeing someone. It is either terrible or great news.

A man asked the librarian for a book on killing yourself. The librarian responded, "Get lost. I know you won't bring it back."

What do you do if a gang of clowns ever attacks you? Go for the juggler.

As recent research indicates, humans do indeed eat more bananas than monkeys. I think they may be onto something because I can't remember when last I enjoyed eating a monkey.

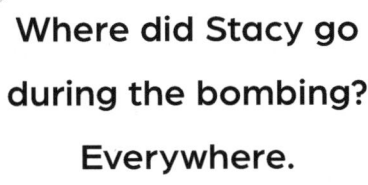

Where did Stacy go during the bombing? Everywhere.

The easiest way to know you are ugly is when you are handed the camera every time there is a group photo.

Why did two Asian parents have an Asian baby? Because two Wongs don't make a white.

My boss farted in front of a Jewish client and then said, "A little gas never killed anybody."

I childproofed my house. Somehow, they still got in.

I remember all the people that I lost as I got older. Maybe a career as a tour guide was not for me.

Wife: I want another baby.
Husband: What a relief! I also really don't like this one.

A son tells his father, "I have an imaginary girlfriend." The father sighs and says, "You know, you could do better." "Thanks, Dad," replies the son. "I was talking to your girlfriend!"

My boss told me to have a good day. So, I went home.

Boy: Mom, can I get a dog for Christmas?
Mom: No, you're getting turkey, like every year!

My husband is mad that I have no sense of direction. So, I packed up my stuff and right.

When I see the names of lovers engraved on a tree, I don't find it cute or romantic. I find it weird how many people take knives with them on dates.

My grandfather says I am too reliant on technology. I called him a hypocrite and unplugged his life support.

When I die, I want to die like my grandfather, who died peacefully in his sleep, not screaming like all the passengers in his car.

The guy who stole my diary just died. My thoughts are with his family.

They say there is a person capable of murder in every friendship group. I suspected it was Dave, so I killed him before he could cause any real harm.

I thought opening the door for a lady was good manners, but she just screamed and flew out of the plane.

My elderly relatives would tease me at weddings, saying, "You'll be next!" They soon stopped once I began doing the same to them at funerals.

Two hunters were in the forest when one of them collapsed. His hunting partner called 911 and frantically screamed, "He is not breathing! What should I do?" The operator responded, "Keep calm, sir. The first thing you wanna do is make sure he is in fact dead." There was silence, followed by the sound of a gunshot. Then the caller asked, "Ok, now what?"

CONCLUSION

And so, dear friends, we have reached the end of our journey of laughter. I sincerely hope that immersing yourselves in the pages of this book has not only made you laugh out loud but also proved to be a great bonding experience for your whole family. As you've delved into the world of humor and laughter together, I envision giggles, shared jokes, and bright smiles filling your home.

I hope that in these pages you've discovered that a simple joke can be the magic spell, that can transform even the gloomiest of days into brighter ones. Jokes aren't just words on paper, they're the threads that bind relationships, and create treasured memories that can last a lifetime.

So keep smiling, keep spreading good cheer, and most of all, in the words of Nissan, remember that "life's a journey—enjoy the ride"

Thank you for joining us on this journey of laughs!

Made in United States
Orlando, FL
19 May 2025

61425172R00055